Dad ,

Love
Colleen.

Merry Christmas 1973.

D0116042

ms
J3
KCU-47037

The Pioneers

The Pioneers

An Illustrated History of Early Settlement in Canada

Introduction by J. M. S. Careless

The Canadian Illustrated Library

FIRST EDITION
© Copyright 1968
McClelland and Stewart Limited

REVISED EDITION
© Copyright 1973
McClelland and Stewart Limited

ALL RIGHTS RESERVED

No part of this book may be
reproduced in any form without
written permission from the
publishers, excepting brief
quotations for review purposes.

The Canadian Illustrated Library

McClelland & Stewart Limited
The Canadian Publishers

ILLUSTRATED BOOKS DIVISION
25 Hollinger Road, Toronto 374

0-7710-0034-0

Contents

Introduction

"Those who gave this country to us"

J. M. S. CARELESS, PROFESSOR OF HISTORY, UNIVERSITY OF TORONTO.

A hard, uncaring land, empty and enormous: this was Canada to the pioneers, whenever they settled. For the fishermen from the West of England, sheltering in coves in 17th-century Newfoundland, endless grey seas spread out before them, forbidding barrens lay at their backs. For the colonists of 18th-century New France, clustered in river-bank cottages along the great St. Lawrence, the Appalachian wilderness loomed on one side, and, on the other, the frowning mass of the rugged Laurentian shield reached off to an unknown north. Even for 19th-century settlers in what would be the fertile farmlands of Ontario, the thick dark wall of the Great Lakes forest arose a hundred feet above them, spelling isolation and straining effort until heavy primeval timber could be cleared away and rows of rotting stumps grubbed out. □ As for the western pioneer of the early 20th century, he might reach the great plains by rail; but there remained a lonely, jolting waggon journey to some distant quarter section of unbroken grassland, while vacant horizons stretched away to the curve of the globe itself. Finally, for the rancher, miner or lumberman of early British Columbia, he above all others experienced the giant size and solitude of Canada, among the soaring ranges, deep valleys and fiords of the far west. Assuredly it was a hard, uncaring land to the pioneer; and its locked-in riches would be paid for in failure as well as success, in emotional stress and cultural setback, as well as in physical hardship. □ Of course, it was not all harsh and forbidding, or few would have stayed. Hope lived constantly with hardship: the promise of a fuller life to be gradually realized, more prosperous and self-determining than that which settlers had left behind. There was land, and room and resources – plenty for all. There was a good chance for well-being and even affluence; and for many also, the prospect of far more scope in a much less restricted society than that of their old class-conscious homeland. □ Nor was the Canadian scene always frowning. In the Atlantic region, there were gentle valleys as well as rugged coasts, placid pastoral settings like the Acadian farmlands in Nova Scotia, the Loyalist homesteads up the beautiful Saint John River, the green fields and deep red soil of Prince Edward Island. In French Canada, Quebec and Montreal were sizable towns well before the fall of New France, with handsome buildings and brightly varied urban life. And even by 1820, Ontario farms in the Bay of Quinte, Niagara and Windsor areas had taken on a well-cultivated look, displaying gardens, orchards and stone or brick houses, as well as fine white clapboard mansions. In the West, the spread of settlement rapidly transformed buffalo prairie into a huge golden granary, while Vancouver rose with the Pacific railway to become a bustling city almost overnight. Pioneers, then, felt the promise and made good the opportunities, to shape modern Canada out of the raw material of half a continent. □ There were many groups of them through the long years of building. There are some still, pushing, probing ever farther into the vast northern expanses of this country. But for the basic pioneering elements, the forerunners of the modern nation, whose lives are recalled in this book, a few main groupings will serve to describe them. To begin with, there were those who arrived by sea, and those who came by land. The first stream brought the French, the British, and other European groups in a great transatlantic migration. The second stream of settlement was most clearly marked by the Loyalists, who came northward from the new United States after the American Revolution. This continental movement would bring many other pioneers from the United States in later eras, and also carry eastern Canadians to help settle the western plains and mountains. □ In the Atlantic migration, the French who came to New France after 1600 to colonize the St. Lawrence valley were first to plant a major European settlement in the future realm of Canada. But New France lived largely by the fur trade with the western Indians; its pioneers were fur-trade venturers and missionaries as well as farmers. As a colony, its growth was limited; few immigrants came from

France to join it after 1700. Nevertheless, this St. Lawrence settlement survived the British conquest of 1760 and continued growing from its own vigorous fertility. French empire and the fur trade might disappear, but the staunch *habitant* farmers of the St. Lawrence would go on pioneering, pushing back bush farms into the rough forested country above the river on into the Laurentians. They would indeed survive, to leave their legacy in the modern province of Quebec, and in French Canadian communities scattered westward across Canada. □ The truest miracle of survival, however, was that of the Acadians, the still smaller group of French colonists who settled in the Atlantic region in the 17th century. These simple farming people built a life of their own around the shores of the Bay of Fundy – and then were expelled and scattered in the 1750s, during the death-struggle for the continent between the French and British empires. Yet they endured, returned and re-emerged, finally to become a prominent factor in the Atlantic provinces, especially in New Brunswick. □ The British elements that came to control Canada after 1760 had, of course, been planted in Nova Scotia and Newfoundland long before; it should be remembered that English fishermen were establishing themselves in Newfoundland when New France was coming into being. In the 1580s in fact, the harbour of St. John's was already thronged with shipping, and the busy path along its shore was taking shape as the oldest street in British America. But the really outstanding age of British pioneering came much later, in the first half of the 19th century. It was in that time that Scots, Irish, English and Welsh settled through the Atlantic provinces, in the Eastern Townships of Quebec (or Lower Canada, as it then was) , and steadily filled in the farming frontiers of Ontario, then Upper Canada. □ These were days when clumsy timber ships carried great squared beams of Canadian timber to British ports and returned crammed with living ballast from Liverpool, Belfast and the Clyde. These were days, too often, of death and horror on the

Atlantic passage, when cholera and typhus raged in the reeking holds of "coffin ships," above all during the terrible exodus from famine-stricken Ireland in the 1840s. Yet for all the dangers and suffering of the long voyage under sail – to be relieved by better regulation and then by the coming of steam – vigorous British immigrants poured in to populate Canada. Scots came to Cape Breton and Prince Edward Island, to the south-western lands of Upper Canada; Irish went to New Brunswick, the Ottawa Valley and the Peterborough district of Upper Canada; the English to counties in that province such as York, Simcoe and Middlesex. But all of them located in many other areas as well. □ The Irish, the majority of them Protestant Ulstermen, were the largest single group in this great migration before 1850. When immigration from Britain resumed in another giant wave from the 1890s to the First World War, English elements were the most numerous. And this time the newcomers went on to settle in a booming West, though they also helped built up eastern cities and industry. Now, however, these British transatlantic migrants moved by steamship and rattling trains of colonist cars – not by the slow barges, *batteaux* and ox-carts of an earlier day. And this time, in the pioneering of western Canada, they were not predominant; but went in company with Canadians, Americans and continental Europeans to develop the prairies and British Columbia. □ The continental Europeans were the newest element in the stream of Atlantic settlement. They arrived in numbers only after 1900, though Mennonites and Germans had been in Ontario much earlier, and Icelanders on the Manitoba plains since the 1870s. In fact, about half a million immigrants came from Europe in the boom years before the First World War, to nearly twice that quantity from Britain. But the European migrants were distinctive in bringing ethnic variety and a host of languages to English Canada and they particularly settled in the prairie West. □ Ukrainians, Austrians and Poles, peasants from the Balkans, artisans from the Baltic,

Dutch, Scandinavians and Italians, religious sects like the Doukhobors – these and still more gave colour and diversity to pioneer life in Canada such as it had never had before. They brought their customs and their cultures, their building and farming practices to variegate the wide sweep of the plains – from the Hutterite farms in Alberta to the many-domed Ukrainian churches in Winnipeg. □ Since our original settlers, the Indians, flowed gradually southward and eastward from a vanished Alaskan land-bridge to Asia, to occupy the tribal lands where Europeans found them so many centuries later, there has always been a flow of peoples across North America and Canada. But let us trace the overland movements only back to the British conquest of 1760. The taking of New France brought English-speaking merchants north from Britain's American colonies to settle in Quebec and Montreal, while New Englanders moved into Nova Scotia, particularly to occupy the farmlands of expelled Acadians in the Annapolis Valley. Yet these limited movements were dwarfed a few years later when the old British colonies broke away in the American Revolution, and many who had backed the British cause there left to seek new homes in the remaining colonies to the north. Loyalist refugees flooded into Nova Scotia and, extending outward, they brought about the creation of the new province of New Brunswick in 1784. Others moved up the St. Lawrence beyond the occupied French Canadian lands, where their settlements – spread from Cornwall to Kingston and Niagara – led to the creation of the province of Upper Canada in 1791. □ Plainly, the influence of these Loyalist pioneers was great. They helped to give a pro-British, anti-American cast to Canada, reinforced by the American attack in the War of 1812 and the arrival of British immigrants in growing numbers thereafter. But the Loyalists nevertheless *were* Americans (of this continent if not "United Statesers") seeking to survive in America. And many of them were experienced frontier farmers to begin with, who readily took up pioneering north of the American border. Moreover, they were followed by many ordinary American frontier settlers, who came into Upper Canada or the Eastern Townships not for any political reasons but essentially because the land was fertile and easily obtained. These post-Loyalist Americans were no less experienced and valuable pioneers in early Ontario or Quebec and, in general, merged easily into the Canadian scene. □ A two-way flow of population across the American border still goes on. We may be conscious in Canada of what we lose by this flow, but we need also to remember what we have gained: in people, skills and enterprise well adapted to open more of the Canadian land-mass. In this way Americans (some of them returning Canadians) took a prominent place in settling the plains of Saskatchewan and Alberta, often bringing with them needed techniques like the dry-farming developed in American western regions. And they moved up the foothills and mountain valleys of the far west to the cattle, lumber and mine frontiers of Canada around the turn of the 20th century. Cowmen from Wyoming, big-tree lumberjacks from Oregon, California prospectors on the Yukon Trail of '98 – they all added still more colour and strength to the Canadian pioneer fabric. □ So much more to mention: the inland Germans who settled Lunenburg in Nova Scotia, and so adapted to the arts of the sea that their descendants could one day produce the supreme beauty of the schooner *Bluenose;* the sturdy Selkirk Scots of the Red River, who withstood armed attack, droughts and grasshopper plagues to found Manitoba; the sports-minded English colonists of Cannington Manor, Saskatchewan, who enjoyed cricket, tennis (with afternoon tea), and even a fox hunt on the open prairie. In all this variety, was there anything common to the pioneer experience? □ Several things, perhaps. First, if Canada was so often harsh, cold and exacting, settlers who won through to reap its resources often managed to obtain a considerable degree of comfortable good living. Game was usually plentiful. Even with the limited labour available, harvests were normally good from newly cropped soils. Except in the earliest years of settlement, pioneers usually ate well – simply but well: a far better diet than their European contemporaries. They could with effort, also be warmly dressed and well housed. When neighbours were near and good sleighing available on frozen rivers or forest tracks, the hard winters were times of cheerful, work-free socializing. Contented security and high-spirited fun could offset heartbreaking failure or the gloom of isolation. □ There was usually a strong sense of community. Success might rest with individual enterprise, but it equally involved joint effort – sometimes work and play combined – in the ubiquitous "bees": logging bees, barn-raising bees, or even apple-drying bees. Family ties were strong, and there was a happy, sure belief in improvement and progress. How could it be otherwise, when a man could see wilderness cleared back, prairie ploughed, log or sod cabins replaced by neat, well-fitted farmhouses–and when the locomotive, traction engine, and farm machines brought the power of the industrial revolution to shrink distance and human toil? The pioneer believed in success and, sometimes, he seemed also to believe in excess – in heavy drinking or fervently hell-fire religion. In any case, drinking freely and praying earnestly, he sweated out his liquor on hard work or in the repentance of the temperance movement. And his faith was real in a just God, a bountiful nature, and the certain worth of individual effort. □ Pioneers simply were people; not heroes or living legends, with seamy faults as well as stalwart virtues. Normally rough, too busy for book-learning or pantywaist culture, they could as well be stupid and selfish in wasting resources, ruining land and destroying tree cover – the settler's traditional foe. Yet, originally, they sought to build for a better future; despite the endless toil and heart-breaking setbacks, they had the strength of hope and vision, a ready warmth and kindness, even a natural courtesy. And they were the forerunners: those who gave this country to us. This book is but a brief recognition of our enduring debt.

They came to Canada

Here begins a unique pictorial record of the arrival of the pioneers – men and woman of many races and many tongues who were caught by a bright promise and stayed to build a nation.

The French

The early arrivals from France, some in wigs and fine yarns, had a lot to learn about survival in Canada. Indians could be friendly or ferocious. Fur traders discouraged colonization. At Champlain's death in 1635 there were only 85 souls in New France; but just over a century later the population was 65,000.

The English

Choosing life under the English Crown to the shaky promises of the new
American republic, 50,000 United Empire Loyalists came north to Canada.
Many left fine homes and thriving farms. Pure English blood was
relatively thin in British Canada – even at Confederation, Scots and
Irish were more numerous in a country ruled by the English since 1760.

The Scots

An "epidemical fury of emigration"
(according to Dr. Samuel Johnson)
took place in Scotland in 1773.
Pictou, Nova Scotia, received the
first of them: 180 Protestant
Highlanders debarked from the
Hector onto free land. The Scots
pioneers brought their stern
religion with them – a gathering
of Covenanters (right) worship in
their new land. Other spurts of
settlement put Scots over the
breadth of Canada, and names like
MacGillivray, Selkirk, Fraser and
Mackenzie opened the land for all.

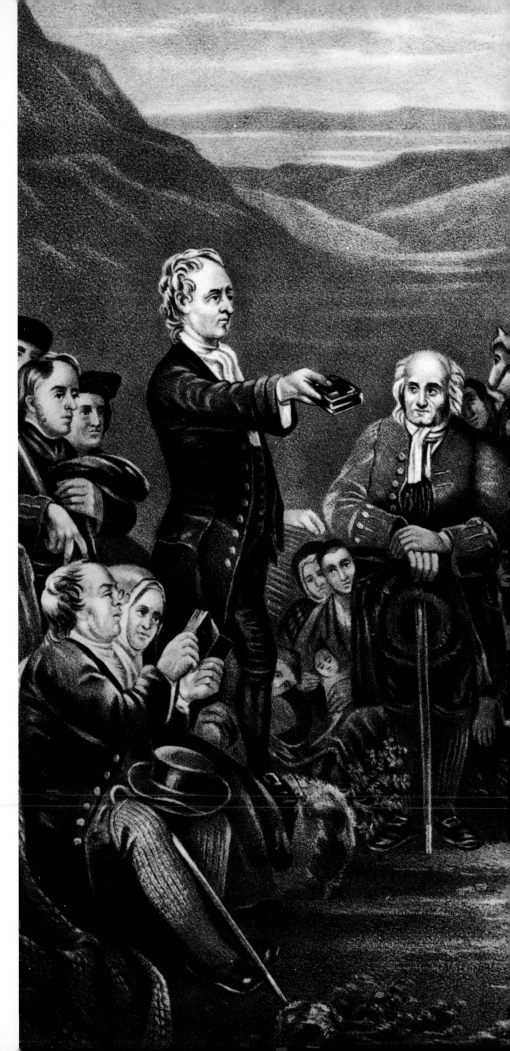

The Irish

The great surges came after the abortive Irish rebellion
in 1798 and after the potato famine of 1864 when 1,600,000
fled. Travelling wretchedly in the dank holds of sailing
ships, the Irish peasants arrived by the thousands and took
mostly to lumbering and clearing the land. Midway in the 19th
century, they outnumbered the Scots and English in Canada.

The Dutch

The Ukranians

The Norwegians

The Poles

The Bulgarians

The Germans

The Austrians

The Finns

Pioneers of the Atlantic Coasts

"The sea remained their friend"

W. S. MACNUTT, DEAN, FACULTY OF ARTS, UNIVERSITY OF NEW BRUNSWICK

Among all of the diverse peoples who came to the Atlantic Provinces – French, English, Scots, Irish, Germans – one characteristic was clear. The sea that brought them to the new lands remained their friend. They clung to the coastal harbours and estuaries of the great rivers, for it was the sea that kept them in contact with civilization, with the supplies they so desperately needed to sustain their settlements, with their homelands in Europe. □ Tidewater stood for security in a harsh, unbroken country. The English settlers of Newfoundland moved along the coast from harbour to harbour. Fishing was their livelihood and they ventured to leave the shoreline only on brief excursions for game. It was more than two hundred years after the first settlement of John Guy that a lone traveller crossed the great island from east to west. In the settling of New Brunswick in the 1780s, the First Battalion of De Lancey's Brigade, a crack Loyalist regiment, refused to accept the block of land that fell to it by lot – near the contemporary Woodstock – because it was too far from the mouth of the St. John River. Even in the small province of Prince Edward Island, where nothing was remote from the sea, Lord Selkirk found it difficult to persuade his Scottish settlers to live away from the shoreline. Dependence on water transport kept the new colonists looking seaward and development inland was slow; not until the middle of the 19th century were the northern areas of New Brunswick and other remote areas invaded by settlers. □ At the outset, when starvation was always a threat, governments frequently assisted the struggling pioneers, but after the first crop the new settlement was on its own. Fish was vital: for several generations the barrel of salted cod or herring tided many a family through the winter. Some were much more fortunate than others. Loyalist settlers of the St. John River with large holdings of interval land became the envy of Scots and Irish who arrived later and were compelled to clear wooded upland. Some had ample pasturage for cattle, others could scarcely sustain a cow. Many made poor choices of places to settle. A cleared field on marginal land could always show a great cairn of stones in the middle, a witness to labour almost vain. Many a forest clearing was quickly restored to bush as it was abandoned by disheartened settlers and the rapidly improvised log hut, insulated by birch bark or seaweed, soon fell to pieces. □ There were always more sections than settlers and many pioneer farmers found it easier to clear new land than maintain the fertility of the old. "Clean-cutting" was the ideal method, pursued by the more industrious – those who considered it worthwhile to save a tree for the value of its timber. But the great majority, strangers to the broad-axe, preferred to burn, growing their crops between the stumps of the great trees until, many years later, they rotted away. Potatoes could be produced quickly after the burning. In the districts that originally were heavily wooded it was only in the second generation that easily plowed fields began to appear. □ Farmers did not understand the uses of animal manure and seldom employed readily available supplies of seaweed and musselmud in nearby creeks. Stunted farm animals pastured in partly cleared forests; according to an account of the 1820s, pigs in Prince Edward Island resembled greyhounds. Thomas Chandler Haliburton ridiculed his fellow Nova Scotians for their preference for raising fine horses rather than fine crops. Too much land, said critical and knowledgeable agriculturists, was given to hay. □ Newfoundlanders never bothered to develop an agricultural industry. Except for the fish they produced, their food was imported. When land was cheap and plentiful, why labour on another man's property? The best farmers, it was often remarked, were those with strong sons who remained on the land, and industrious daughters who stayed home to spin and weave. □ Seasonal employment on the farm or in the fishery became more diverse when, during the Napoleonic Wars, timber became a staple export. Even in communities by the sea, where men cultivated small garden plots and fished from schooners of twenty to thirty tons, they were seduced to the backwoods by lure of greater returns. A winter of enterprise and excitement in the far reaches of the navigable rivers became the common lot of thousands of younger men. In the spring, when the work of the great timber drive was completed, they emerged for a festival of frolicking and merry-making, to the great trepidation of the people of the seaport towns. Saw-mills of all sizes squared the timber for export. □ It was not until the 1820s that "the great roads," with their corduroy beds and rickety wooden bridges, enabled traffic to flow continuously away from the coasts. In the summer, woodboats patrolled the rivers, taking to market the slim surplus produce of the settlers, bringing in the hardware and small luxuries of the outside world. Winter was the season of rapid transit in most areas. The frozen rivers and snow-covered roads made easy going for sleighs. Great loads of hay, potatoes and other farm produce could be readily conveyed to centres of population like Halifax, where garrisons of imperial troops, small industry and overseas shipping made markets. □ Always there were hazards. The pioneer annals of the Atlantic Provinces are full of tragic tales of shipwreck, privations of the settlers in the forest clear-ings, the burnings of towns and the ravages of great forest fires that could terrorize an entire countryside. The Miramichi fire in October, 1825, was the classic example. This great holocaust destroyed 5,500 square miles of timberland – nearly one-fifth of the province of New Brunswick – and four prosperous towns, all constructed of wood, were reduced to ashes.

28

The Pierced Rock

Percé Rock, situated two leagues south of Gaspé Bay with its arch nearly 60 feet high, has always been a Canadian landmark. Early settlers in the Gaspé Peninsula, and all of the early explorers who sailed down the St. Lawrence River, saw the Rock with two arches as depicted in this engraving from a sketch by Captain Hervey Smith, one of Wolfe's aides. Smith served aboard the Vanguard, a ship of 70 guns, shown here passing the Rock in 1760. The second arch collapsed in 1853, leaving only a single arch to mark the passage into the interior of Canada.

Footholds of Settlement

It took a lifetime to make a dent of settlement on the hard coasts of the Atlantic. A fort like Port Royal (1605) could be quickly established, but the habitations and farms behind them were longer taking root. When the first settlers came they hacked their farms from the virgin forest and burned the logs to fertilize the land. Two hundred years later, when Patrick Campbell Esq., a gentleman traveller toured old Acadia, he drew the fanciful – but informative – picture *(at right)* to illustrate how things had prospered since Samuel de Champlain founded his Habitation on the Bay of Fundy. Campbell noted four types of fence –"Virginia rail, worm, log and post-and-rails"– a Dutch barn, a residence shingled with bark, and the winter cattle shelter. He also included himself in the picture *(in canoe, with hat)* and turned the friendly Indians into gondoliers.

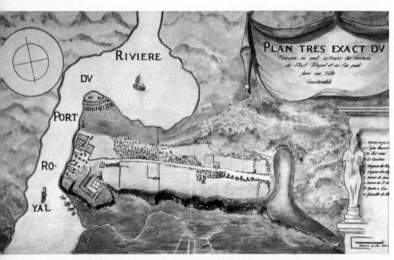

By 1686 a French map could show farms rising near Port Royal.

Ft. Lawrence (1755): cannon protects the spreading cornfields.

A town is born in the wilderness

Many pioneer communities just happened – at a river ford, or at the end-of-rail – but some were created by businessmen, as suburban developments are today. Stanley, New Brunswick, began that way in 1835 as a project of the New Brunswick and Nova Scotia Land Company. The incompetence of its officials killed the company, but Stanley survives to this day, on Highway 107 just 30 miles north of Fredericton. The stage-by-stage illustrations on this and the following pages were prepared, like a modern publicity brochure, to lure the adventurous immigrant. They did, too.

1 The site for Stanley was chosen by surveyors where the line for their road met the scenic Nashwaak River.

2 The new town's first need was a saw-mill, and to power it they built a dam of logs laid at right angles to each other and weighted with stones. The structure at the left is the framework of the flume that will bring the water to the mill wheel.

3 The finished dam, with the mill yet to be built. Provisions for the work crews were hauled upriver in dugout canoes, some 36 feet long. The trip was so arduous a horse would last only two seasons, and the drenched boatmen got rheumatism.

4 At the townsite, the construction superintendent spent his first season in a wigwam shingled with spruce bark. His floor was spruce boughs covered with a buffalo robe and his only furnishings a teakettle, a tin dish, and a pannikin.

Overleaf: Smoke from burning trunks and branches fills the air as the land is cleared for the first crop, invariably a big yield from the virgin soil.

A smiling land beckons

Two years after the land was bought in 1833, the town of Stanley was a fact. Thirty-four acres of forest were cleared, a crop already taken off, and the road pushed 23 miles farther north to meet the Miramichi River. A new community had been created in the wilderness.

The saw-mill sent its lumber down the Nashwaak River to markets.

In August, 1835, the ready-made town was ready for occupancy.

◁ The most imposing edifice in the town was the tavern; room charges included hay for your horse.

Getting around

Wheels were not all that much use to the early pioneers: there were no roads to roll them on. The carts of the day were clumsy but strong, solid birch, their wheels bound with iron. In winter, things ran smoother: sleighs everywhere, from one-dog toboggans through rude farm sleds to elegant town *carrioles*. The rivers, the lakes and the sea, these were the real roads then – and the ingenious settlers developed a boat for every purpose.

Newfoundland dog pulls a toboggan.

The common farm sled.

An ox-cart with iron-bound wheels.

Two-seat family sleigh.

A gentleman's town sleigh.

Overleaf: In its earliest days St. John's was merely a convenient sheltered base from which the Newfoundland fishery could be conducted. 17th-century British legislation discouraged settlement to ensure that youthful trainees in the Newfoundland fisheries would return to England where they would be available for service in the Royal Navy. Despite this opposition, settlement did occur. Early immigration was largely Irish, and by the end of the 18th century they outnumbered the English. Although the harbour is small it is deep and so landlocked that the water is always calm, an ideal refuge from raging ocean storms. Signal Hill, on the north side of the harbour, is the highest point in the region. The plate on the next page shows a view of St. John's from this vantage point.

Cutter carrying British soldiers.

Lumber-hauling "Johnny Woodboat."

Birch-bark canoes.

A flotilla of canoes.

Newfoundland: treasure from the sea

Before Columbus, the first English adventurers seeking gems and spices skirted the northern coasts of America: they found the silvery codfish instead. By the end of the 16th century, settlement of Newfoundland was underway – the first clearing house for the first produce of the New World.

For centuries, Newfoundlanders went out in their dories in all weathers to the ▷ Grand Bank. Today, a single catch by net has been known to weigh 1,000 tons.

An early (1710) drawing shows the dry-curing method used by the English at shore settlements. The French salted and barrelled their catches at sea.

Women work on the "bawn" (a beach used to dry fish) of St. Pierre, off the coast of Newfoundland. It has been a French settlement for nearly 300 years.

The harsh reality

This is the face of early settlement in Canada: stark, grim, but determined. This is how New Denmark, New Brunswick, looked in 1873. A year before, seven Danish families and ten single men arrived and began to clear the 150 acres each settler had been allotted. The trees are gone now, and houses are built, but this early photograph from the New Brunswick Archives reveals what the sketch-pad of romantic artists obscured – the disfiguring stumps still clutter the fields, the gaunt settlers strain to straighten their toil-bent backs and spread themselves out, perhaps to make the group look larger. Somehow, the old print shows also the fortitude, the silent heroic tenacity that was the mark of the pioneer. For New Denmark *did* survive. Today it's part of a rural community of hamlets with a population of 1,750. These same heart-breaking fields are now smooth and sleek and fertile.

Pioneers of New France

"Every Canadien a tough guerrilla fighter"

W. J. ECCLES, PROFESSOR OF HISTORY, UNIVERSITY OF TORONTO

The French first came to America as adventurers, not settlers. They were seeking a route to the Far East and supplies of precious metals such as the Spanish had discovered in Mexico. Failing in these aims, they eventually turned to trade in furs, and this in early years brought handsome profits. The Indians produced the furs, ready for market, in exchange for European goods like knives and blankets, pots and pans. All that was necessary was to maintain good commercial relations with them. There was no need for a large, settled population. ☐ In the beginning, then, ships sailed each summer to trade with the Indians at Tadoussac on the lower St. Lawrence, returning in the autumn. But as more and more ships came to trade, competition became fierce and profits declined markedly. The obvious way to meet the problem was to establish permanent year-round trading posts further up-river. In 1608 Samuel de Champlain founded such a post at Quebec. ☐ From these beginnings, settlement slowly grew. When the first missionaries arrived at Quebec in 1615, they brought settlers to till the soil and reduce dependence on food supplies from France. The fur trade interests also brought out some settlers for the same purpose. Moreover, within a few years the clergy founded schools, hospitals, even a college at Quebec (preceding Harvard by one year) and, before the end of the 17th century, alms houses for orphans and the aged poor had been built at Quebec and Montreal. New France became a veritable welfare state. A colonial council and law courts dispensed justice cheaply, swiftly, and equitably. In fact, the pioneer Canadians grew extremely fond of litigation: haling one's neighbour into court over some petty dispute soon become the second most popular indoor sport in the colony. ☐ During these years the colony was under constant attack by the Iroquois. Soldiers were sent from France and a number of settlers came for religious reasons, like Crusaders of old, to help bolster the defences of the missionary outpost. Far to the west, in the Huron country by Georgian Bay, the major mission centre of Saint Marie was established – only to be soon abandoned because of Iroquois pressure. Gradually, despite the danger and frequent setbacks, the hardwood forest along the shores of the St. Lawrence was cleared. Colonists took up land as tenants on large tracts or seigneuries granted for settlement. The river offered an easy means of communication to the people of the seigneuries. Thus their farms, over the years, became narrow strips running back from the river with a house on the water's edge – and every few miles, a seigneurial manor house, a mill, and a parish church. ☐ At first, the homes of the pioneers were little more than wooden huts, surrounded by stump-pocked fields. By the mid-18th century their houses were of stone with steep roofs, reminiscent of northern France. In the early years these *habitants*, as they became known, had had to struggle desperately hard to survive. By the 1720's, however, they were, compared to their counterparts in Europe, relatively affluent. Their seigneurial dues and church tithe were very low, and they paid no taxes. Virgin land could be had for the asking, they enjoyed the right to hunt and fish, and every *habitant* family kept horses which were used for sport and social occasions as much as for working the land. ☐ Although agriculture was the backbone of French Canada's economy, the fur trade was still its life blood. Every year hundreds of tough-fibred men voyaged far inland to trade at distant posts. From Montreal they went by canoe, laden with trade goods, to the Mississippi Valley, across the great plains to the foothills of the Rocky Mountains, or north over the Laurentian Shield. Others from Quebec, no less adventurous, sailed down the St. Lawrence on sealing and whaling expeditions, with cargoes of flour and lumber to the Atlantic fortress of Louisbourg or the West Indies and, in war time, on privateering voyages. And down the Ottawa and St. Lawrence to the French settlements came the western Indians to trade their furs and discuss policy with the colony's governor-general. ☐ Along these river routes stood virtually every house in the colony. Thus the French pioneers were a people of very broad horizons, accustomed to travel over the continent, mingling constantly with the Indian nations, adopting something of their way of life. These influences quickly made of them a people very different from those of Europe. The Iroquois threat in the early years, and that of the neighbouring Anglo-American colonies in the 18th century, obliged every Canadien to be a tough guerrilla fighter. ☐ From 1685, a large corps of French regulars was stationed in New France. The commissioned ranks were opened to the sons of Canadian seigneurs and they responded eagerly. The values of the officer corps, based on those of the French nobility, became dominant for the upper class, and for those who aspired to enter that class. Thus rank, personal honour, valour, were regarded as far more important than middle-class virtues of thrift, prudence and industry that came to prevail after the British conquest of 1760. Partly for these reasons, partly owing to geographic factors, industry and the arts did not flourish in New France. Some industries, such as ship building, lumbering, iron forging were established, but mainly to supply local needs. ☐ The typical Canadian in the days of New France was a man who in his youth voyaged to the west and lived among the western tribes for months, perhaps years, went on military expeditions against the Iroquois or the English colonies, farmed his fifty to a hundred acres on the banks of the St. Lawrence, spoiled his children after the fashion of the Indians, set a hearty table, raced his horses, dismayed the curé with his wild parties and the luxurious dress of his women folk at Sunday mass. There was little of peasant sluggishness or bourgeois stability about this society. Rather it was dominated by the profligacy of the soldier and the recklessness of the frontier. And while the old frontiers of French Canada might disappear with the British conquest, there would long remain the hardy Canadian *voyageur*, thrusting deep into the north and west in the service of English enterprise, while the robust *habitant* pioneer continued to expand the lumbering and farming of Quebec, in bush clearings reaching far back from the great St. Lawrence artery.

48

Louis Hébert dared the Iroquois to plant wheat outside the palisades. He left a son and two daughters – ancestors of hundreds of today's French Canadians.

First settler, first city

New France's first true settlers, a former apothecary to French royalty named Louis Hébert and his wife Marie, led the tough breed that established the colony. First at Port Royal with the Sieur de Monts, later with Champlain at Quebec, Hébert put down roots and prospered. In 1623 he was farming the land where the Upper Town of Quebec City now stands. In all the French regime's 150 years, not more than 10,000 settlers came from France, yet they established the French Canadian people. The capital city grew slowly, harassed by the Iroquois and even occasionally by the English. When the freebooter David Kirke captured the settlement in 1629 it had only 65 colonists, and eleven years later the entire French population was still only 240. Yet the city on the rock in the St. Lawrence had already established the Jesuit College (1636, a year older than Harvard), the Ursuline nuns had started a girls' school, and the Hôtel Dieu hospital was founded on the site it still occupies today. By the beginning of the 18th century, Quebec was a gay colonial capital, the seat of a bishop, a bustling centre of commerce, and the bastion of French sovereignty in the New World.

The capital of New France, astir with river traffic, looked like this in 1722, according to an old engraving. That year, 85 parish governments were established.

QUEBEC

A. Le Fort
B. les Recollets
C. La plate forme
D. Les Jesuittes
E. La Cathedralle
F. Le Seminaire
G. l'Hostel Dieu
H. L'évéché
I. La Redoute
K. Le magasin a poudre

A French village 4,000 miles from France

This reconstruction of Ste. Marie-among-the-Hurons is a replica of the French mission established on this site deep in Huronia in 1639, a thousand miles from the Jesuit headquarters in Quebec. Tragedy stained its brief life, for the Iroquois, armed with Dutch muskets, invaded the land and martyred five priests caught outside the walls. While it lasted, Ste. Marie was a strange, brave experiment in the wilderness: a French village of French-style buildings, sheltering priests, a surgeon, a tailor, and the inevitable soldiers. Today, tourists walk through the buildings and climb the nearby hill to pray at the shrine of the Canadian martyrs.

The rebuilt Ste. Marie stands near Midland, Ontario, on the Wye River, on Georgian Bay. As many as sixty-six Frenchmen lived in the fortified bastion (below, right); the Indians camped in and around the narrow end.

Corn dries in the rafters of the kitchen, built by French-Canadian workmen using tools and methods of three hundred years ago.

The vaulted Huron longhouse could house twenty families. Firewood stood in cones; meat froze or dried on high cribs, safe from dogs.

Ambitious towns of the 17th century

The first need of a town in New France was a fort to protect the settlers from the raids of the Iroquois. Until 1665, the first *habitants* dared not go outside the walls except in groups, and the confined settlements grew so haphazardly that in 1672 Governor Frontenac was complaining of Quebec's lack of a master plan. Montreal's first streets were so narrow – only 18 feet – that traffic congestion was already chronic in the late 1600s. Drunken horse-driving became so serious that a law was passed against it in 1749, with a fine of three *livres* (about six dollars).

Three Rivers was fortified in 1634, but grew ▷ only slowly. After a hundred years it had only 25 houses – and 18 of them were taverns.

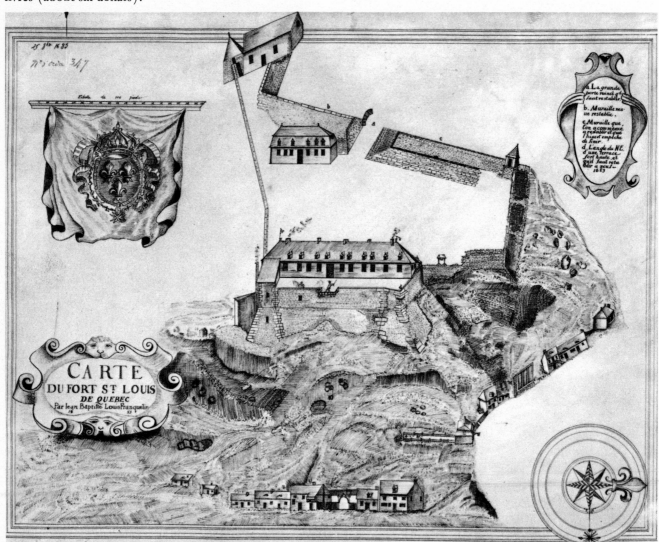

Quebec's Fort St. Louis was still unfinished in 1683. Instead of completing it, soldiers increased their pay hiring out to farmers.

Montreal really got under way in 1644 when ▷ Louis XIV granted the Civic Charter. Thirty years later the population reached 766.

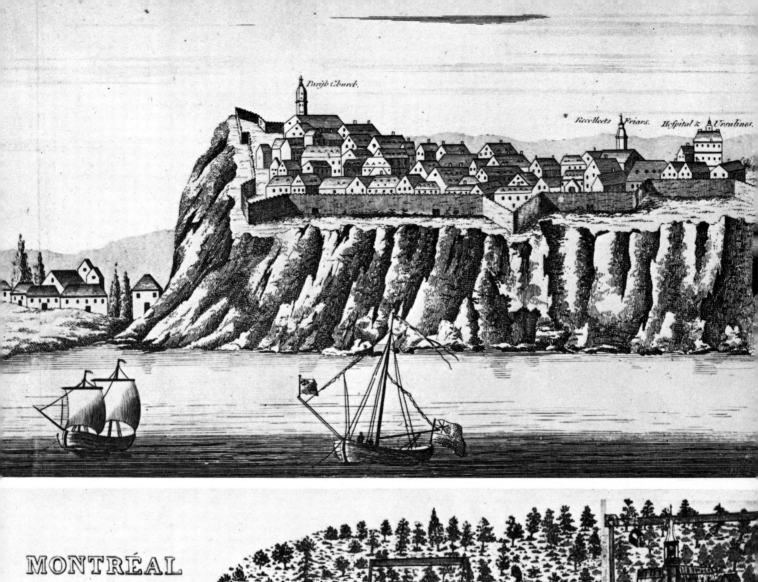

Parish Church.

Recollets Friars. Hospital & Ursulines.

MONTRÉAL

VU À VOL D'OISEAU
de
1645 à 1650.

Rivière St Pierre

St. LAURENT FLEUVE

Ilot Normandin

A

C

B

La Fondation de Montréal date du 18 mai 1642

La première construction faite à Montréal était une clôture de palis située au élévé actuellement la nouvelle Douane.

A. Le Fort construit en 1645, était un quadrilatère régulier, avec quatre bastions en maçonnerie qui se flanquaient très bien. Cette fortification, dont les courtines étaient en bois, mesurait 50 toises de front (320 far) et 2 toises de haut. L'intérieur contenait une chapelle, un hôpital, des logements pour les colons et la garnison, on y eleva aussi des magasins d'un trepot, et près du Fort, on établit le premier Cimetière (E.) ouvert à Montréal. Ce Fort fut démoli en 1672.

B. L'Hôtel Dieu fut fondé en 1642, à la Pointe à Callière. En 1644 on construisit cet Hôpital sur les rues St Paul et St Sulpice, le premier bâtiment qui fut élevé à la jonction de ces rues avait 60 pieds de longueur par 24 de largeur.

C. Résidence de Mr de Chomedey & de Maisonneuve, premier Gouverneur de Montréal, bâtie en 1642 et occupée en 1669 par quatre prêtres missionnaires du Séminaire St Sulpice de Paris qui arrivèrent à Montréal en 1657.

D. Moulin à vent construit en 1648.

Montreal was founded on the 18th May 1642.

Big and sturdy houses for big and sturdy families

Despite early hardships, the *habitants* prospered and multiplied. From a tiny group numbering only 240 in 1640 the population had soared to 10,000 by 1685 – and no woman lacked a husband. One woman named Marie Denot was married three times, and her daughter twice – they had a double wedding on Jan. 26, 1655. To shelter the large families they raised, the *habitants* needed big houses; the first they built were like the ones they had known in France – half-timbered, the walls packed with rubble and stones. Unsuited to Canada's harsh winters, they gave way to sturdier dwellings of stone with walls four feet thick, huge chimneys to

heat them – stoves didn't come until nearly 1700 – and the space inside just one big room, later divided into bedrooms. There was no glass for the windows – even in town – and greased paper was still used for the windows of farm houses as late as 1749. Dishes were mostly wooden, and until the beginning of the 18th century, settlers ate with their fingers and brought their own knives when invited out for a meal. Dishes of earthenware and metal became more common, and sawn lumber replaced stone for houses, particularly in the growing cities, where a single building – often roofed with tin – would frequently include both residence and business.

Overleaf: While the French were content to cling to their traditional strip farms the English were only too eager to settle the empty and promising interior of Quebec. Settlements like the one at Stanstead gave the English a strong foothold in French Canada.

Wealth from the woods

The great natural resource of Lower Canada was its trees and, every winter, it seemed that half the male population went into the woods to cut in preparation for the spring log-drives on the rivers. So great was the timber demand after Napoleon cut off England's usual supply from the Baltic – not only for pine spars for English men-of-war, but for timber for every purpose – that the lumberjacks raced up the St. Lawrence, the Ottawa, and other rivers, levelling the white and red pine, the white oak and other hardwoods. The timbers were hewn square with axes, the better to fit into the holds of timber transports, often hulks too old and leaky to carry anything else. This practice left the forest floor littered with chips where disastrous fires frequently got their start.

The rafts of squared timbers were big enough to live aboard, while shooting the rapids down to Quebec City where the craft were dismantled for shipment.

Some of the womenfolk still worked at the home loom, while the men were away in the tall woods. A jack's monthly wage was $30 in 1880.

◁ *Logs were hauled to the frozen rivers and, when the ice buckled in spring, all hell broke loose. Many Irish shantymen had never before seen a true forest.*

Cards appealed to the Québecois – they liked to mystify the children with tricks as well as play the games themselves. Whist was popular by 1850.

Backwoods life and laughter

The *habitant* life was a satisfying one of hard work and hard play. Their taxes were light, their obligations few, their land productive, even though they dumped their barnyard manure on the river ice instead of on their fields. Their most famous chronicler, Cornelius Krieghoff, painted their life a shade gayer than it may have been, but on the whole it was a good one. As Krieghoff demonstrates on this and the next five pages, winter was the best time for fun in Lower Canada. With a cellar full of cabbages and turnips, a granary full of wheat, a shed full of barrels of frozen beef and game, and a reassuring woodpile beside the house, the settlers could relax and enjoy life. There were religious fests, endless gossip, visits with neighbours, friends and relatives. Krieghoff found town life bright with wit and laughter, filled with gay excursions to such places as Montmorency Falls, nine miles from Quebec, when 15 or 20 colourful *carrioles* would travel to the ice cone, their passengers cuddled into buffalo robes trimmed with fox tails. The clergy disapproved of this sort of conduct, to no effect. The people were religious but never pious – a century before Krieghoff's time the stern Bishop Laval·could not thunder the ladies out of their fondness for elaborate *coiffures* and scandalous *décolletage*.

Schools were important in French Canada; learning wasn't. Bishop Laval founded a trade school in the mid-1600s, but in 1686 it had only 34 boys. Not until Krieghoff's time (1850s) did training in such Christian virtues as humility and obedience give way to practical matters like reading and writing.

A pleasure and a penance

Caught eating meat in Lent, a habitant family cowers before priestly disapproval. The clergy were strict: they opposed dancing, cards, jewellery, even hair ribbons; they were powerful: they could excommunicate a man on the street – but they kept French Canada free of the witch-hunts that plagued New England during that period.

Habitant farms progressed from a rough log hut to a traditional house with a steep roof and bell-skirted gables. The furniture inside was sturdily beautiful, but water came from a hole in the ice in winter. High birth rates encouraged pioneering: in the 30 years after the British conquest, the population jumped from 60,000 to 160,000.

Those winters of content

Longueuil – a ferry ride across the river from Montreal (an ice-bridge drive in ▷
winter) – had a rail link to New York by 1850. The figures in the box-like
red berline are Krieghoff's wife Marie Gauthier (they never formally married),
their daughter Emily, and Gautier père.

Toll roads were common in 19th-century Lower Canada and the gates so
frequent – sometimes only three miles apart – that they became a grievance.
The toll was only sixpence per vehicle in 1849, but running through without paying was a popular game among the young sports.

Quebec and Montreal had their elegant salons, but the simple pleasures of a
sleigh trip to a country inn for a night of dancing and drinking, then a
tipsy return home bundled in toques and furs appealed to the pioneers.

Pioneers of Upper Canada

"A formidable supply of elbow grease"

C. M. JOHNSTON, PROFESSOR OF HISTORY, MCMASTER UNIVERSITY

The Algonquin hunter and the Iroquoian cultivator were probably the original inhabitants of southern Ontario, that triangle formed by the Ottawa, the St. Lawrence, and the lower Great Lakes. The French appeared in the 17th century, but mainly used the region as a "vestibule of trade" through which a supply of western beaver pelts could be shipped out to the St. Lawrence. The change to British rule in the 1760s did not greatly alter the life of fur trade posts on the Niagara or Detroit Rivers. Twenty years later, however, the coming of the Loyalists after the American Revolution brought the first substantial settlements in the area. □ Some of these adherents to the British cause were long rooted in English-speaking America. Others, Scots and Germans, were more recent arrivals in the New World. But most of them were soldiers and farmers from the backwoods of the old colonies, well adapted to a life of pioneering. When they arrived in strength, the region known after 1791 as the Province of Upper Canada struck out on a new course. With rough-hewn ploughs and harrows and a formidable supply of elbow-grease, these determined settlers made the first inroads on the fur trade wilderness. So much so that by 1796 officials in England could observe that, "Trade cannot now be carried on, to any great Extent on the Eastward of the Lakes." □ Though they had just cause to be proud of many of their accomplishments, not all those known to posterity as Loyalists might have recognized themselves in the heroic tradition that a later generation gratefully wove about their exploits and sacrifices. It is conceivable that many who hurriedly departed the former English colonies might in time have come anyway to the fertile lands and strategic carrying-places that abounded to the west of old Quebec. And certainly many who came after them, in the years down to the War of 1812, were simply American frontier farmers seeking the good new land freely granted them by the officials of Upper Canada from the days of the first governor, the enthusiastic John Graves Simcoe. □ Yet some obviously emigrated to Upper Canada because they feared their religious faith or political convictions might be compromised by association with republicanism. This was particularly true of pious and hard-working Mennonites and the full-bearded Tunkers, or River Brethren, from Pennsylvania, who became familiar figures in the western valleys of Upper Canada and worthy contributors to its agricultural and commercial development. And another group, made up of displaced British officials and military veterans set out for the "northern dominion" simply because they had no choice in the matter. Some like Butler's Rangers settled the Niagara Peninsula, others moved into the eastern sections of the colony and organized flourishing communities on the north shore of the St. Lawrence and Lake Ontario. Standing out conspicuously were the Empire's Indian allies, the people of the storied Six Nations of the Iroquois, who had shared in defeat on the battlefields of the American Revolution. Even before Upper Canada was brought into existence these Iroquoian exiles had established "buffer states" along the Grand River Valley and the shores of the Bay of Quinte, adding to the diversity of early Ontario. □ The strong anti-Yankee sentiments expressed by Loyalist newcomers prompted a visitor to observe that "it is common to hear, even from the children of refugees, the most gross invectives poured out against the people of the States." "I am inclined to think," he mused, "that this spirit will not die away while Canada forms a part of the British Empire." These victims of a lost cause had become in many cases more royalist than George III and more loyal than those "true-born" Britons who, according to one outraged settler, harboured unaccountably "no spark of resentment against the Americans." □ A love-hate relationship with a Mother Country which could allegedly forgive and forget so readily, and out-pourings against the United States, sometimes left little room in the Loyalists for a genuine affection for their adopted community. But in time it grew—strengthened particularly by the War of 1812, and the defence of new-won farms and villages against American attacks from the Niagara Peninsula to the upper St. Lawrence, and even at the little capital of York, the future Toronto. □ Following the war, the most important period of British settlement began for Upper Canada. The earlier American settlers, Loyalist or post-Loyalist, were now well established. It was chiefly British immigrants who cleared frontier farms in the Huron Tract, around Lake Simcoe or the Karwartha Lakes, and Irish especially who worked in the lumber shanties of the Ottawa. But the life of the backwoods was not greatly different from what it had been in Loyalist-American days—at least until the coming of better roads, and then the railway in the 1850s, ended inland isolation and linked the filling countryside with rising towns. Hard slogging work in the bush was relieved by trips to the mill and tavern at the nearest "four corners," or by the excitement of mass religious camp meetings. Pioneer life was homespun clothes and wandering peddlars with pots, geegaws and news of the outside world. But it was also pride in spreading fields and fattening stock, and a faith in the fruits of industry that built Ontario.

Preserving the past

The pioneer past is slipping from living memory in most parts of
Canada, but it can still be found in sturdy buildings, rugged furniture,
kitchenware – even children's cherished toys. "Living museums,"
like Upper Canada Village near Cornwall, Ontario, and Black Creek,
15 miles north of Toronto, are carefully preserving pioneer buildings
(by collecting, dismantling and rebuilding them), and furnishing
them with the very plates and spoons dented in use a century ago.

A well-appointed town kitchen of the middle 1800s had one of the
new cast-iron stoves, the first labour-saving gadgets, and china dishes.

A country kitchen with open-hearth cooking had a fireside settle
that opened into a bed for the children who tended the fire at night.

The period look: buildings moved from other sites surround the log houses ▷
built by Daniel Stong at Black Creek in 1816 and 1832.

The fine bed was imported, but the rug was handmade, and so was the gay patchwork quilt – finished at a spring quilting bee.

Wondrous items to grace a pioneer home

By the middle of the 19th century Upper Canada had foundries to make stoves, potteries for crocks and dishes, shoe factories, furniture makers, weavers, tinsmiths, and companies that produced everything from waggons to churns, and the lengthening railroads were bringing the manufactures of the world to cities and towns. People who could afford them could indulge in almost as many labour-saving gadgets as any visitor to an exhibition today – and probably find them no more useful.

Nothing tasted better than home-made butter; this churn was made in Aylmer.

A fancy "cathedral" stove heated drawing rooms or ballrooms in 1840.

Weight-operated clock was imported from Portsea, England, about1845.

Pioneer houswives laid out a whole dollar for this hefty egg-poacher.

Coffee grinder from a general store; pioneer homes had smaller models.

"Fashion plate" showed men's suit styles available from York's tailors.

Simple, hand-cranked sewing machine made a woman's work a little lighter.

Sharp woodworking tools and at least a handyman's skill were essentials.

Wide rim of painted footbath kept water from splashing on the floor.

But the backwoods farmers still had to depend on their own skill and ingenuity. They made their own tools and implements of wood and iron: Joseph Abbott, the father of Prime Minister Sir John Abbott, made the sleigh he courted his wife in, as well as rakes, hoes and harrows. The women were as self-reliant as the men – some of them still wove their own cloth on home looms from wool or flax to make clothing, blankets – even window curtains – and the rags were saved to make rugs for the floor. But when a pedlar came from New York or Rochester with clocks and toys and gimmicks, he found a ready market among the pioneers, some of whom bought just to encourage him to come that way again with his marvellous wares – and tales – from the outside world.

Indians grew our first tobacco; these clay pipes used burley plug.

This jack-in-the-box was labelled "Salt" to fool the pioneer kids.

Brass scales weighed raisins, spices sweetmeats at mid-19th century.

The great outside world became real on Donaldson's New Terrestrial Globe.

When the handle was turned, surprise! The clown became a flower. Date: 1876.

What is it? A stuffed canvas hen? No, a tea cosy once found in every parlour.

The gadget in front cut sugar from a rock-hard lump for the tray behind.

Canada was not yet born when this bread slicer was cutting lunches.

A forgotten way of life: the household water filter on the sideboard.

Expensive toys for well=to=do=kids

There were two kinds of toys – the very expensive toys (like those on these pages) which few children ever saw, and homemade dolls or waggons. Most pioneer boys and girls made their own – log cabins of notched sticks for the boys, and rag dolls for their sisters. But wealthy towns-folk imported toys that were beautiful and imaginative.

The European dolls were replicas of adults – the baby doll wasn't invented before 1850 – and were dressed more fashionably than their owners. Doll houses were elaborate and tin soldiers followed the tradition of the Thin Red Line. The pioneer era ended in 1887 when Irish-born Timothy Eaton brought out the first Christmas mail-order catalogue.

Toys from the Percy C. Band collection at Ontario's Black Creek Pioneer Village show children's delights of the 1800s.

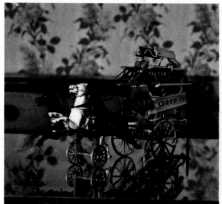

Capturing the eternal excitement of a fire, hook-and-ladder tolled its bell.

Cow is papier mâché inside, but its painted hide is made of real leather.

Paper tigers were star performers in this lively table-top circus.

China doll of 1870 wore the latest fashions. It was filled with sawdust.

Mechanical toys like this woodchopper were highly prized, but very dear.

Wooden hobby-horse had real mane and tail. Some even had real fur hides.

Most kids were stoking real stoves, not playing with doll sized ones.

This carved Indian doll was made by the Snake Island Indians about 1850.

Alcohol-burning steam engines were almost too valuable to play with.

The magic lantern brought exciting glimpses of wondrous, far-off places.

Hand-carved horse and waggon is the toy most pioneer boys would have.

Iron locomotive (about 1880) was of a type then called "fast express."

Elizabeth Simcoe

Anne Langton

Susanna Moodie

Well-bred women from the Old Country took some shocks in pioneer Canada that rattled their British phlegm. Even the Governor's lady dined on moose-lip and lived under canvas.

Three literary ladies: they wrote it all down and illustrated it too.

Elizabeth Simcoe left a luxurious estate in England when her husband, John Graves Simcoe, was appointed first Lieutenant-Governor of Upper Canada, and moved into three tents on a hillside at Niagara in 1792 until the official residence could be completed. She contributed her share of gossip to the tight little settlement, but she found just about everything to be worth a page in her diary. She ate black squirrel (it tasted like young rabbit), accepted a pair of rattlesnakes in a barrel and wrote down an antidote for their bite (pounded crayfish applied to the wound). She lived in a two-room "canvas house" – a boarded-up tent – when the capital was moved to York in 1794 and the Simcoes' nine children used one room and the other was the Governor's bed-sitting room and office. Mrs. Simcoe was polite but often reserved in public; the Duke de la Rochefoucauld said she was "timid, but a woman of sense." In her diary she called him "perfectly democratic and dirty – I dislike them all." Her only other dislikes were the heat and the mosquitoes, and when she returned to England in 1796 she took with her a Canadian sleigh, a canoe and paddles, bows and arrows, and some Indian clothing, and kept them until her death in 1850 at the age of 84.

Anne Langton joined her bachelor brother John at his farm on Sturgeon Lake near Fenelon Falls in 1837, and she stayed with his family until she died at 88 in 1893. Her schooling in Switzerland and Rome didn't prepare her for life in the bush – going without soap, running out of candles and lamp oil (as they did in 1838), helping to butcher cattle and cut up the meat in the farm kitchen, learning to bake her own bread, and putting up with the cold. With the family homestead and farm well established, Anne taught the children of other settlers to read and write. Her monument is her journal: A Gentlewoman in Upper Canada.

Susanna Moodie's first home near Cobourg in Upper Canada in 1832 was a miserable hut with one window. She saw it first during a torrential September rain, with a crying baby in her arms and a wailing servant girl at her side, and not even her husband there to soften the blow – he was two miles behind her with their baggage in a waggon. "My love for Canada," she wrote of that time in her book, Roughing It In the Bush, "was a feeling very nearly allied to that which the condemned criminal feels for his cell – his only hope of escape being through the portals of the grave." Before she died in Toronto aged 82 in 1885 she was able to write: "May the blessing of God rest upon Canada and the Canadian people." In the intervening years she had been cheated by landlords, survived a forest fire, eaten chipmunks and subdued her pride to work like a man in the fields. "I have contemplated a well-hoed ridge of potatoes on that bush farm with as much delight as in years long past I had experienced in examining a fine painting."

Spinster Anne Langton drew this candle-dipping machine in her sketchbook, fifty years before home electricity was available.

Elizabeth Simcoe

Before photography, sketching was a military
necessity and Mrs. Simcoe was able to use soldiers'
drawings to portray places she never saw.
Places she did know, like Castle Frank, her home
on the Don River, she painted again and again.

Anne Langton

Her ladylike sketches reflect Miss
Langton's pleasure in the compar-
ative sophistication of her communit
Of the six settlers on Sturgeon
Lake in 1833, four were university
graduates, the fifth an officer, and
the wife of the sixth played the guita

Mohawk Village, near present Brantford, was based on a sketch by one of Simcoe's aides.

Castle Frank had a Greek portico supported by unbarked pine trunks. It burned in 1829.

Susanna Moodie

Sketching wasn't Mrs. Moodie's strong
suit, but her flat style caught the
desolation of trees killed by the sulphur
roasted off ore from the Marmora
Iron Mine from 1820 to 1873.

Ferguson Duke's farm near Fenelon Falls, 1840.

Pioneer miners pickaxed hard magnetic iron ore for wages of $24 a month in 1826.

The Langton family; that's Anne by the fire.

Workers at Marmora lived in these cabins in 1837; four owners were ruined in 40 years.

Gold fever in Hastings County

Gold was discovered on the farm of Mr. John Richardson in 1867. The presence of gold in the area had been known by the government for several years previous to this but it had been leary of letting the information be made public. The assumption that gold was not present in renumerative quantities and fear that an undesirable class of persons would be attracted to the area induced the government's caution. This caution was shattered by the Richardson

find as speculators rushed into the area by the hundreds. For two years the excitement continued and just as quickly it petered out. Except for the perseverance of a few men, interest in gold mining was soon abandoned. A few enterprises like the Gatling gold mine (below) proved to be of value and were worked profitably for a number of years, but by the end of the century the district had entirely reverted to its more certain pursuit of agriculture.

One man's impressions

In 1844 Titus Hibbert Ware, barrister of the Middle Temple in London, England, visited Canada with the intention of practising law near Orillia, Ontario. Apparently he did not stay but he did keep a diary of his visit in which he described the country, the price of land conditions of the roads and frontier society. He also made thirty-four pen-and-ink sketches and watercolours which, along with his diary, give an excellent picture of the pioneering spirit of Upper Canada.

Log house stands amidst the newly cut trees.

Corduroy road over a swamp in Orillia – composed
of logs laid side by side to permit travel in what
would otherwise be impassable mud.

Before engines made it easy

With only the horse and block-and-tackle to help them, the early builders accomplished prodigious works, like the first Welland and Rideau canals, both in operation by 1832. They used sharp wits too – to begin the first suspension bridge at Niagara in 1851, kites were flown over the gorge, then rope was attached to the kite-string, then, finally, the first cable was pulled across.

Parliament Buildings now stand on the bank where the Rideau\Canal begins its 123-mile journey (47 locks) to Kingston, on Lake Ontario.

Homan Walsh's kite won the contest in 1848 to carry a string over the Niagara gorge for Charles Ellet's suspension bridge, at Lewiston.

Britain was hungry for timber. How to get it to Quebec? The answer was the ▷ raft of squared logs, steered down timber "slides" by the lumberjacks.

Pioneers of the Western Plains

"This encounter of land and people" ·

L. H. THOMAS, CHAIRMAN, DEPARTMENT OF HISTORY, UNIVERSITY OF ALBERTA

Lieutenant William Butler had called it "the Great Lone Land" when he travelled by horseback from Fort Garry to Fort Edmonton in the autumn of 1870. Yet he was confident that the awesome solitude of the plains and parklands of the Canadian North-West would be dispelled by a wave of migration destined "to convert the wild luxuriance of their now useless vegetation into all the requirements of civilized existence." This same expectation was shared by the Fathers of Confederation and, following the union of the eastern provinces in 1867, Canada had moved swiftly to acquire the territory between Ontario and British Columbia from the Hudson's Bay Company. That the region had great agricultural promise seemed clear enough but the territory was so vast that its true character could never be revealed except by men and women strong and adventurous enough to test and subdue it. This encounter of land and people was the essence of the pioneer experience. □ Like Lord Selkirk's colonists at the Red River two generations earlier, the first homesteaders settled within sight of trees – they provided fuel and building material and, moreover, there was a suspicion that the open plains were arid and unproductive. In the Seventies, the parklands in the vicinity of Manitoba's lakes, and the North Saskatchewan Valley, were believed to be the best areas for settlement. The well-worn cart trail running north-west from Winnipeg to Edmonton gave access to this country, and the launching of steamboats on Lake Winnipeg and the Saskatchewan River was expected to guarantee adequate transportation until railways could be built. But, by the time the Canadian Pacific Railway was incorporated in 1881, enthusiasts were claiming that there was scarcely an acre of poor soil between the Red and the Rockies. □ The C.P.R. staked its solvency and the prosperity of thousands of homesteaders on a route far to the south of the Saskatchewan Valley. This was sod-house country, wind-swept, bleak in the wintertime, and monotonous. Yet the soil was productive, if rains fell during the growing season. At ten-mile intervals, a railway siding gave birth to a village, with its unmistakable wheatland profile of a line of elevators against the skyline. "No. 1 Manitoba Hard" began to move into the export trade in the 1880s, establishing a world-wide reputation for Canadian prairie wheat. But success sometimes eluded the sod busters, with drought, frost and grasshoppers taking their toll. For many, there was more money in gathering buffalo bones, and freighting supplies during the Rebellion of 1885, than in growing wheat. Some left the country in despair. □ But there were good years too – more good than bad – enough, anyway, to nourish

patience and optimism, the most notable traits in the prairie mentality. Pioneer families graduated from riding in back of the crude unsprung waggons with the bagged wheat or the month's
store groceries, to the buckboard and then – some of the luckiest or most industrious – to the
carriage or the "surrey with the fringe on top." □ The route adopted by the C.P.R. shattered the
expectations of the first farmers in the Saskatchewan Valley and postponed settlement there for
nearly twenty years, but it was a boon to the ranchers of the Chinook belt of southern Alberta.
The arrival of the North West Mounted Police a few years earlier had ended the turbulent enterprises of the whisky traders; this, and the signing of Blackfoot Treaty No. 7 confining the Indians
to reserves, stimulated the importation of range cattle from Montana over the Whoop-Up Trail.
Ex-traders and ex-policemen were the first ranchers, but they were soon joined by young Englishmen for whom life in the shadow of the Rockies had an irresistible appeal. The 1880s were the
heyday of ranching, with vast acreages under lease; thereafter the interests of the homesteader
were given priority and grain growers encroached, often unwisely, on land which should never
have been turned by a plough. □ Extraordinary efforts were made to promote immigration and
by the time Ford's "Tin Lizzie" was replacing the horse, two million pioneers were on the land.
Ex-Canadians were repatriated from New England factory towns (where many *Québecois* had
settled) and from the mid-western States. Mennonites were lured from southern Russia with
assurances of respect for their communal and religious interests, as were Mormons from Utah
and Jews from Eastern Europe. In 1898, seven thousand Doukhobors arrived. Icelanders escap-
ing from volcanic eruptions were promised a colony of their own. Ukrainians responded to the
lure of free homesteads, joined by Scandinavians, Germans, Hungarians, and others. With the
arrival of Scots and Englishmen – and even a few Welshmen who abandoned a strange colony in
Patagonia – the older society of Indians, whites and *Métis* became a veritable patchwork quilt
of cultures. □ The present style and way of life on the Prairies – those elements that distinguish
the plainsman, and woman, from other Canadians – were set in pioneer days. The loneliness of
a prairie wife, with the nearest house clear over the horizon, made simple neighbourliness essen-
tial. Families imported from a hundred different backgrounds, in a dozen different countries,
set out eagerly to create new communities – bare and bleak maybe, to an eastern eye, but full
of warmth and tolerance and, indeed, of something that might pass for universal brotherhood.

Most immigrants came steerage, like these Germans in 1874. Fare was $30.

The tide flows west

Until the coming of the steamships in the 1860s, the voyage across the Atlantic in leaky sailing ships was a nightmare for most of the homesteaders bound for the limitless acres of the Canadian West. A passage could take six weeks, or sixteen, and immigrants died in shipwreck and of starvation. Steerage accommodation on the steamships was an improvement but there was no privacy – 16 bunks to a "pen" was common in 1879 – and the night was hideous with drunken noise, retching and the cries of children.

After 1858, an Allan Line ship, subsidized by Canada, left Liverpool every week crowded to the rails with European emigrants.

Well-dressed British settlers – more than one-third came from the United Kingdom – wait at the immigration sheds in Quebec. At times, foreign tongues drowned the English and (see sign) the money changers were ready to do business in all currencies.

More than two-and-a-half million settlers came to Canada between 1903 and 1914. The railway was the magic carpet that bore them westward. These Scotswomen left Quebec for the Prairies with whisky bottles full of milk for the children. Scots still make up eleven per cent of the population.

Beyond the reach of rail

Railways opened the West – the last spike of the C.P.R. was driven on November 7, 1885 – but every pioneer had to solve the problem of getting from the nearest station to his land in his own way. A good waggon fetched $175 at Winnipeg in the 1880s, and even a squeaking, jolting, Red River cart was worth $20. Paying the freight was impossible for most: it cost $168 to send 100 pounds the 460 miles from St. Paul to Fort Garry in 1882. When the trail ruts got too deep, the *Métis* carters simply put one wheel up on the fresh sod. In this way, the trail across the plains from Battleford to Edmonton got to be twenty ruts wide.

Mormons came from Utah in covered waggons to settle south-western Alberta, in the 1880s. By 1912, nearly a million Americans had followed them.

Ox-hauled waggons could make ten miles a day over the prairie. Horses could travel 30, but oxen were cheaper, more reliable – and edible.

Edward Smith (hand on hip) and his sons Jack, Joe and George trekked in ▷ 1907 to Heatherwood, Alberta – the foothills centre later renamed Edson.

The river as a road

The western rivers had always been the highways of the Indians, explorers and fur traders, but they were at first a barrier to most settlers, who came by land. When the steamboats arrived, freight rates from Winnipeg to Prince Albert dropped to four cents a pound, and passengers paid $15 – if they slept on deck. Cable ferries were soon strung across most of the major rivers.

Pride of place goes to these pioneers who sailed from York Factory to the Red River settlement in 1812 in sturdy double-ended York boats.

They'd use anything that floated: this log raft was photographed on the Peace. "Bumboats" were made of moose hide over willow frames.

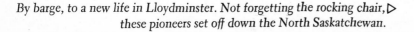

By barge, to a new life in Lloydminster. Not forgetting the rocking chair, ▷ these pioneers set off down the North Saskatchewan.

"They went to ground like a gopher"

On the windswept treeless plains, the settler's first dwelling was dug from the ground – walls of sod on a frame of precious poplar or willow. Grasses and wildflowers still grew on the roofs, and canvas usually hung in the windows. Firebreaks were ploughed to protect the homestead against the grass fires which were touched off by lightning or a locomotive. Buffalo bones worth $6 a ton, were often the first crop.

Of a sod house, a pioneer wrote: "A three-day rain outside meant a five-day rain inside." The lure was 160 flat acres for free.

Where there was timber, log cabins arose in a dozen designs. John Wood built this comparatively luxurious home. The smoke pipes locate his sheet-iron stoves, used for both heating and cooking.

Ukrainians from the Austro-Hungarian provinces of Galicia and Bukovina brightened the prairies, not only with their verve and energy, but with their houses – plastered with clay and brightly painted, like this one between Yorkton and Edmonton.

Peopling the Prairies

A homestead rises

So fast did the plains fill up that an old timer was anybody who had been a year in one place – long enough to learn how to fleece the newcomers, like the colony of greenhorns led from England by the Reverend Barr. When 1,437 of them arrived at Saskatoon on April 17 and 18, 1903, the storekeepers doubled their prices. The colonists didn't even have tents to sleep under — the Immigration Department supplied them, and showed the inept men how to pitch them. Some had never harnessed a horse or driven a waggon and, to save his toes, one man stood in a wash tub while chopping kindling, only to have a chip fly up and strike his eye.

The land: Ernest Brown took these pictures near Edmonton in 1906.

The Barr colonists, many of them Cockneys, paused at Saskatoon en route to Battleford.

The clearing: The trees came down and, by June, the foundations were in.

The frame: As work pushed ahead in the summer, the family camped on the site.

Christened Regina in 1882 – formerly, it was "Pile of Bones" – the new capital of the N.W.T. had a two-year-old paper, the Leader, by 1885.

The home: By late fall the roof was on and everything secure against the snow

First fruits

"I think a stalwart peasant in a sheep-skin coat, born to the soil, whose forefathers have been farmers for ten generations, with a stout wife and a half-dozen children, is good quality."

— CLIFFORD SIFTON, MINISTER OF THE INTERIOR, 1896-1905.

A woman's day was never done

Twenty-four hours were too few for the sturdy pioneer women. Most of them worked in the fields, pregnant or not, and spent their nights weaving linen, cotton and wool to make clothes. They struggled to master some English so that they could start their children on a "reader." Some stayed alone, miles from neighbours, while their man "worked out" to make money to buy a cow or a team of horses.

Before she could bake bread in her clay oven she sometimes had to cut, thresh and grind the wheat for her flour. This photograph was taken in 1905 when the provinces of Alberta and Saskatchewan were created.

Doukhobor women separate the wheat from the chaff by hand-winnowing. When they lacked draught animals, these immigrants from Russia harnessed themselves to the plough.

The snorting conquerers of the plains

The giant steam tractors came with the 20th century – enormous machines whose rear wheels towered six feet high, steel-cleated, with treads five feet wide. Some weighed 20 tons and could pull a 14-furrow plough; with a blacksmith to keep the ploughshares sharpened, they could work 24 hours a day. In the fall they pulled the threshing caravans to harvest the wheat. At last, the worst of the back-breaking toil was past and the hard wheat from Canada began to flow like a golden river. In 1908, fourteen thousand men travelled west for the harvest, some from as far east as the Maritimes, and often made as much as fifty dollars for a sixteen-hour workday.

With a steam-powered Reeves pulling ten ploughs, a man could turn over 100 acres of prairie sod a day.

Before tractor power took over, oxen started ploughing at 3 a.m., then quit at 10 to avoid the exhausting midday heat.

Some settlers were unlucky enough to hit stones; laboriously they hauled them out and dumped them in the nearest slough.

Horse and tractor co-operate in this threshing outfit near Wetaskiwin. The first mechanical reaper appeared as early as 1831.

When the steaming behemoths weren't breaking sod, they powered threshing machines. They bowed out in the late Twenties.

Horseplay at
harvest time

Pioneer kids made their own fun. Life was sweetest on Sunday afternoon, when chores and studies were put aside for fooling around in the barnyard, trapping gophers or looking for crow's eggs. When neighbours called it was time to show off tricks practiced in private (*see below*). It was also the day that the older sons went courtin' in the pony-and-trap.

If the rains came and the wind didn't flatten them, oats grew taller than a ten-year-old. Later, science shortened the stalks to withstand wind.

The sporting life

Once, in 1894, the Manitoba legislature couldn't obtain a quorum – the members were at a bonspiel. In 1896 Winnipeg won the Stanley Cup with a high shot on goal known as "the Winnipeg Scoop." Just about every slough was a winter rink and, in summer the bolder belles appeared in the daring swim suits of the day.

Ice hockey swept the Prairies in the Nineties. This extemporaneous team from Saskatchewan had four McPhees – Mary, Donald, Little and Big Angus.

The English tradition of cricket, lawn tennis and croquet was maintained by this team at Wolseley, Saskatchewan. But baseball had already made a beginning in the West.

For this picnic at Round Lake, in 1910, the menu was: hard-boiled eggs, home-cured ham, cold roast chicken, a bucket of potato salad, home-made bread and butter, raisin pie, and cold tea. And they ate every crumb.

A saucy siren of 1893 models her ▷ bathing costume at popular Lake of the Woods, where Manitoba, Ontario and Minnesota meet. The first cottagers' association there was formed in 1881.

Signs of sophistication

How grand was Winnipeg! But, alas, when this montage photograph was manufactured in 1883, society was not yet quite this splendid. Following a fad of the period, the figures were all photographed separately, then pasted on a background grander than anything the pioneer metropolis could provide. But the city did have two dashing regiments – the Winnipeg Light Infantry and the Winnipeg Rifles – and an historical and scientific society already four years old. The Dramatic and Literary Association, and the Philharmonic Society, had been founded in 1876, but they both foundered when the leading lights, Mr. and Mrs. E. Brokovski, returned to the East.

Pioneers beyond the Rockies

"Stampeders who settled a wilderness"

MARGARET A. ORMSBY, HEAD, DEPARTMENT OF HISTORY, UNIVERSITY OF BRITISH COLUMBIA

At first, it was the search for sea-otter skins and for beaver pelts that lured men to the North-West Coast and the ubiquitous Hudson's Bay Company created a fur preserve west of the Rocky Mountains. To fight off American competition, the company built Fort Victoria in 1843 and six years later sponsored the colony which the British government decided to establish on Vancouver Island. Around Fort Victoria and at the Nanaimo coalfield there gradually clustered about 400 Scottish and Canadian fur-traders, Hawaiian and French-Canadian employees, English colonial officers and country squires, Staffordshire miners and a few journalists and professional men. □ Suddenly, this tranquility was shattered forever by the discovery of gold on the Fraser River in 1856. Governor James Douglas acted quickly to preserve the vast mainland territory from American seizure when 20,000 miners raced up in a fleet of stern-wheelers from San Francisco. Victoria, the placid English hamlet, became a tent-city in the spring of 1858; Americans, French, Germans, Mexicans and Chinese swarmed onto the mainland and swept away the monopolistic privileges of the H.B.C. □ The feverish panning for gold on the bars of the lower Fraser disturbed the quiet fur-trading operations at Fort Langley, Fort Hope and Fort Yale, and trade shifted from these solitary posts to new villages and to the mushrooming port of Victoria. Meanwhile, the search for the mother lode pushed the miners onward into the interior of British Columbia. By 1862 their picks and shovels were unearthing the treasure of the Cariboo: more than $50 millions in gold was eventually won along the Fraser. □ To help Governor Douglas maintain order, the British government sent law officers and a detachment of Royal Engineers to British Columbia. The troops laid out a colonial capital on the Fraser River at New Westminster, and marked out other towns. When roads became essential, the Engineers and others constructed the Great North Road, connecting Yale at the head of navigation on the Fraser with Barkerville in the Cariboo diggings. □ The 600-mile Cariboo Road, the first great engineering feat in the mountainous interior, opened trade and travel between the coastal settlements and the remote goldfields. Freight-trains, stage coaches and the "gold escort" travelled its rattlesnake grades and ominous heights. Men walked its length to take up farmlands, or to find employment in constructing shafts for the deep diggings. Bankers, lawyers and clergy were drawn to boom-town Barkerville – and so were saloon-keepers, card-sharps and dancehall girls. □ The pattern established in the pioneer Cariboo would be the pattern of British Columbia's future: later mineral strikes in the interior would cause great excitement and "stampedes" of prospectors.

Mountainsides would be stripped of their evergreens to provide mining lumber as well as whip-sawn timber for houses in new communities. Under pressure to open transportation routes, daring engineering would solve communication problems in the high mountains. And each excitement would leave behind it a residue of permanent settlement. ☐ The gold fever subsided in 1866. Much of the mobile, polyglot population dispersed, but gold-seekers who now wanted to have a stake in the country turned from mining to cattle-ranching in the Chilcotin, Thompson, Nicola and Okanagan valleys, or to mixed farming on the Fraser River delta. The mainland and island colonies were united in 1866, but the high cost of clearing townsites and building a great highway had left British Columbia debt-ridden. In 1871, the 10,000 colonists—most of them British in origin—turned to union with Canada to solve their problems. ☐ Prosperity was long in coming. But soon after the last spike in the C.P.R. was driven in 1885 and the west coast connected to the cities in the east, the "Terminal City" of Vancouver had grown to five thousand residents. Every boat and train now brought new settlers: lumbermen and loggers, fishermen and cannerymen, capitalists and labourers, bankers and brokers, lawyers and news-papermen. Steamships unloaded China tea and Oriental silks on Vancouver's docks; stands of giant timber near Burrard Inlet provided lumber for the South American and Australian trade; and wholesale grocers reaped fortunes by selling commodities to the sockeye-salmon canneries on the Fraser and the Skeena Rivers. Vancouver boasted electric light and the telephone. Victoria, growing more slowly, retained its early character of a typical English provincial town and benefitted from winning the seat of government. ☐ Pioneers swept into the interior with more solid prospects than the "stampeders" of early decades. Towns like Golden, Revelstoke, Ashcroft and Kamloops had taken on new life with the coming of steel. Settlers with capital began to acquire great holdings of agricultural lands, as well as timber leases and mineral rights. Retired Canadian businessmen, English public-school boys and the younger sons of noble English families purchased fruit ranches. Coal discoveries fired the development of East Kootenay. By 1896, British and American capital was pouring into silver-ore and gold and copper-ore mines, and the cities of Nelson and Rossland were springing to life. The Klondike gold rush two years later intensified interest in the west coast's resources. ☐ By the turn of the century, the Vancouver boom was well under way, and it continues to this day. British Columbia, young in historical terms, still stirs with the lively, reckless spirit of its gold-rush days.

Into the green kingdom

The settlement of British Columbia was always a story of trees and mountains. When the frantic scrabbling for the gold of the Fraser subsided, settlers began mining the greater riches of the interior – to carve out farms, ranches, and the less glamorous ores of the cordilleran ranges. The towering firs crashed to start instant lumbering empires. The pioneers followed the Cariboo Road, that daring 18-foot wide million-dollar highway winding and soaring from Yale to Barkerville. By the time the colony beyond the Rockies joined the rest of Canada to the distant east, the population had leapt to 36,247, and nearly 9,000 of them were white.

Prince Rupert grew from this tent camp to a city in four years, then withered when the C.N.R. moved the new network's headquarters to Vancouver.

Richfield's miners slashed every stick of timber for shacks and sluices, then had to put cabins on pilings to escape the flash floods that followed every rain.

A road gang pushes slowly through the forest of Vancouver Island – this photo- ▷
graph was taken near Quatsino. It sometimes took three days to survey a mile.

In, on, and around the giant trees

The Pacific rain forests are still the source of British Columbia's greatest wealth, and Douglas firs more than 200 feet high are still waiting to be felled, although the spectacular giants of the early days – some 350 feet high – are gone. When these pictures were taken in the 1880s, timber leases cost as little as one cent an acre, and land was leased by the square mile. Even after a reform law was passed in 1888, leases still went for a nickel an acre. The forests were so thick the lumbermen felled trees by the nine-pin method: they cut the smaller trees halfway through, then felled a giant on top of them, and as much as 20 acres went down crash!

Below: Vancouver's tree house stood where 4230 Prince Edward St. is now. It had a kitchen in the stump at right, a living room at left, with a bedroom above it reached by a ladder.

The trees were immense. The stump on which these pioneer couples are dancing measured twelve feet across.

This tree stood on what is now Georgia Street, Vancouver – between Granville and Seymour. Alex Russell felled it Feb. 12, 1886.

Vancouver then and now

Where Spratt's Oilery (left) – it made fish oil to lubricate the skids over which oxen dragged fir logs to water – stood in 1884, the neo-classical Bentall Centre (below) soars three hundred feet today.

The Columbia Brewery (left) stood at the very edge of the forest at Cedar Cove in 1892. The site today is the north side of Powell Street (above), between Wall and Victoria Drive.

Hardly more than a century ago – in 1862 – Vancouver's first three settlers, William Hailstone, Sam Brighouse and John Morton, arrived, looking for potter's clay. They bought 550 acres beside what was to be Stanley Park for £114 11s 8d and were called greenhorns for their stupidity in buying so far (twelve miles) away from New Westminster. But it was an inspired purchase and their lots became the West End of Vancouver. The city was incorporated in April 1886, and on a clear sunny Sunday the following June it burned to the ground in 45 minutes, killing at least a score of people, including a family who escaped the flames in a well but died of suffocation. Vancouver rose again around its first civic centre – a maple tree where Carrall, Water, Powell and Alexandria Streets now meet, and on whose trunk the notice of its first civic election was posted in 1886. By then it had a population of 5,000 and a real downtown office building. On Aug. 8, 1887, its streets first blazed with 300 electric lights, and in 1891 English journalists could report that no one would think of building a house without a telephone.

From byway to highway

Granville Street, Vancouver, today (above) looks like any modern four-lane road; in 1895 it wasn't more than a track in the tall timber, (see photograph, right) with hazards all its own. On the night of Dec. 23, 1895, during a wild westerly gale, a tree crashed into the road on top of a nine-passenger stage coach. The horses and Japanese passengers escaped unhurt but the driver, Walter Herbert "Billy" Steves, was killed on this spot at the crest of Summit Hill.

The rise and fall
of a crossroads

When Angus Fraser's house (above) was built at the turn of the century, the intersection of Cordova and Carrall Streets was close to Vancouver's business heart. Today the area is reverting to its pioneer past as conservationists move in to rescue the remaining 19th century buildings (left) from their fate as war-surplus outlets.

118

Where shall we have the picnic?

Why, in 1,007-acre Stanley Park, of course – and if you didn't
go there by boat in 1888 you had to walk in, for the road
encircling it was still a year away. The favourite spot, then as
now, was Chaythoos, once the site of a Squamish Indian
village, and now called Prospect Point. It was the largest and
best grassy spot in all the Government Reserve, as the area
was originally called. It wasn't reserved for a park though; Col.
Richard Moody set it aside for a gun emplacement if
Vancouver should ever be attacked by sea.

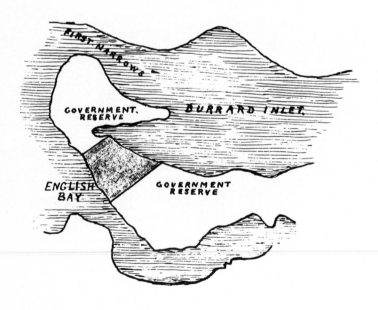

*Picknickers were already flocking to Vancouver's Stanley Park
(right) a year before its dedication in 1889. The crude drawing
(above) was the first map filed to keep the peninsula for the Crown.
In 1960, a statue was erected to Governor-General Lord Stanley, who
had officially changed it from a military reserve to a public park.*

A whiff of the wild west

The artery that gave life to British Columbia was the Cariboo Road, built in three years – 1862-65 – to open an all-weather route to the goldfields on the upper Fraser. The new road cut the $360-per-ton freight costs, and was so well made the Cariboo Stage could take it at full gallop; when it thundered past, the mule trains and their cumbersome waggons stood at the very edge of the precipice to give it right of way. It took five days to go the 300 miles from Ashcroft to Barkerville by stage, but the fare was so high – $50 – that many a miner preferred to walk.

Frank Barnard started his express company by carrying the mail 400 miles ▷ on foot. His first stage ran from Yale in 1863.

Mule teams hauled three tons of supplies into the interior. Grand pianos and cases of champagne went up the road to Barkerville.

The Royal Mail stopped at 100 Mile House only long enough to get a fresh team of six horses, then galloped to the next stop, 18 miles on.

The stage coach had no springs; it hung on heavy leather straps. When the ▷ gold was coming out, guards "rode shotgun."

Below: Dogs haul a barrow of luggage along the main street of Dawson. The gold strike on the Klondike in 1896 brought the town a population of 25,000 – now dwindled to a mere 800. The Yukon capital was moved in 1952 to Whitehorse, 340 miles south.

Wake Up Jake's was a Barkerville hot spot. The Fire Brigade ball in 1875 lasted two nights.

Fernie prospered on "black gold" – coal – dug to fuel trains climbing Crowsnest Pass.

At Atlin, near the Yukon border, in 1901, dogs delivered drinking water from the lake.

The get rich towns

Gold lured men into the wilderness beyond the Rockies as nothing else could – a miner at Williams Creek wrote home in 1862 that he was making $3,000 a day – and for each new strike a new town was born. They were rowdy and raucous, but never lawless – the pioneer magistrates saw to that, often with on-the-spot justice: one dispute was settled with a foot race. And where the men went, women followed, including the German hurdy-gurdy girls with their red waists, printed cotton skirts and insatiable demands for gold. The miners danced with them in saloons, swinging them heels-to-ceiling like bells. There was refinement, too – in Barkerville, French, German, Latin and Greek lessons were $12 monthly.

Overleaf: On your marks!
Dawson's fire brigade, on July 1, 1902.
Three years earlier, while the firemen
were on strike for higher pay, the town
caught fire and 117 buildings were
burned to the ground for
a loss of more than a million dollars.

Picture credits

Order of appearance in the text of pictures listed here is left to right, top to bottom. After the first recording, principal sources are credited under these abbreviations: Glenbow Foundation GF / Harvey's Studios HS / John Ross Robertson Collection JRRC / Manitoba Archives MA / National Film Board NFB / New Brunswick Museum NBM / Notman Collection NC / Public Archives PA / Selwyn Pullan SP / Saskatchewan Archives SA / Toronto Public Library TPL / Vancouver Archives VA / Peter Varley PV / Bud Watson BW / Webster Canadiana Collection WCC / Harold Whyte HW

1   John Ross Robertson Collection, Toronto Public Library
2/3   New Brunswick Museum
4   Dudley Witney
5   Dudley Witney
6/7   Public Archives
15   Giraudon
16/17   JRRC, TPL
18   PA
20/21   PA
22   PA
23   PA
24   TPL; PA
25   PA
28/29   JRRC, TPL
30   Webster Canadiana Collection, New Brunswick Museum; WCC, NBM
31   WCC, NBM
32   WCC, NBM, HS
33   WCC, NBM, HS; WCC, NBM, HS; WCC, NBM, HS
34/35   WCC, NBM, HS
36   WCC, NBM, HS
37   WCC, NBM, HS; WCC, NBM, HS
38   WCC, NBM; WCC, NBM; WCC, NBM; WCC, NBM; WCC, NBM

39   WCC, NBM; Beaverbrook Collection, NBM; PA; PA
40/41   JRRC, TPL
42   New Brunswick Archives
44   A History of Newfoundland, Macmillan 1895, by D. W. Prowse
48   PA
49   PA
51   Bud Watson; BW; BW
52   PA
53   WCC, NBM; WCC, NBM
56/57   JRRC, TPL
58   Notman Collection
59   NC; NC
60   National Film Board
61   NFB
62   NFB
63   National Gallery of Canada
64   NFB; NFB
65   NFB
68/69   Peter Varley; PV, Harold Whyte
70/71   HW
72   PV
73   HW
(Toys and artifacts on pages 70 through 73 were photographed with permission of Black Creek Pioneer Village, Toronto. Toys are from the Percy Band Collection, donated by the Robert Laidlaw Foundation)
74   PA; Courtesy E. C. Guillet from The Pioneer Farmer and Backwoodsman; PA
75   PA
76   PA; PA; PA; PA
77   Ontario Archives; Ontario Archives
78/79   JRRC, TPL
80   JRRC, TPL
81   JRRC, TPL; JRRC, TPL
82   JRRC, TPL; JRRC, TPL
83   JRRC, TPL
86   PA; PA; PA
87   PA; PA
88   GF; PA
89   GF
90   PA; Stephenson Albums, United Church Archives

91   Alberta Government Photo, Ernest Brown Collection
92   PA
93   PA; PA
94   Saskatchewan Archives; SA
95   Alberta Government Photo, Ernest Brown Collection
96   PA
98   PA; Manitoba Archives
100   SA
101   SA; SA; GF; SA
102   PA
103   PA
104   SA; SA; SA
105   MA
106   Miller Services
110   Vancouver Archives; British Columbia Archives
111   VA
112   VA
113   PA; VA
114   VA; VA
115   Selwyn Pullan; SP
116   SP; VA
117   VA; SP
118   VA
119   VA
120   PA; VA
121   PA; Canadian Pacific Railway
122   British Columbia Archives; VA; L. M. Rose Collection
123   PA
124   PA
128   Stephenson Albums, United Church Archives

Acknowledgements

For their assistance in gathering illustrations for this book, the editors thank especially John Sloane of St-Marie-Among-the-Hurons Museum, Dr. George MacBeath of the New Brunswick Archives, and Father Cormier of the Acadian Museum, University of Moncton

A note on the authors

J.M.S. Careless

wrote the Introduction to this book and edited the contributions by his expert colleagues. Now 53, he was Chairman of the Department of History at the University of Toronto 1959-1967. Educated in Toronto and at Harvard, he served during the war as a special assistant to the Department of External Affairs. He won two Governor-General's Awards for his books, *Canada: A Story of Challenge*, and *Brown of the Globe*. Most recently, he published *Colonists and Canadiens 1760-1867*.

W.S. MacNutt

is Professor of History and former Dean of the Faculty of Arts, University of New Brunswick. Born in Charlottetown, P.E.I., in 1908, he studied at Dalhousie and took his M.A. in England. He served in the Canadian Army as a captain in World War II. A Fellow of the Royal Historical Society, he has written widely on Maritimes history, including *The Atlantic Provinces, 1713-1867*, and *New Brunswick: A History*.

W.J. Eccles

English-born, Montreal-educated, has made the history of New France his especial field. After taking his Ph.D. at McGill University, he studied for two years at the University of Paris. Now 55, Dr. Eccles is Professor of History at the University of Toronto. He is author of *Frontenac, the Courtier Governor, Canada under Louis XIV, The Canadian Frontier, 1534-1760* and *France in America*.

C.M. Johnston

lives at Ancaster, Ontario, near the campus of McMaster University where he is Professor of History. He was educated at McMaster and at the University of Pennsylvania (Ph.D.) and is a past member of the Archaeological and Historic Sites Board of Ontario. His books include *The Head of the Lake: A History of Wentworth County, The Valley of the Six Nations*, and *Brant County*.

L.H. Thomas

Professor of History at the University of Alberta, is 55. Born in Saskatoon, he graduated from the University of Saskatchewan and took his Ph.D. at the University of Minnesota. He was editor of *Saskatchewan History* journal for nine years. He is the author of *The Struggle for Responsible Government in the North West Territories*, and a former Provincial Archivist of Saskatchewan.

M.A. Ormsby

Professor Margaret Ormsby, author of *British Columbia: A History* is Head of the History Department at the University of British Columbia. She is a Fellow of the Royal Society of Canada, past-president of the Canadian Historical Association, and a past member of the Historic Sites and Monuments Board of Canada.

THIS BOOK WAS WRITTEN, EDITED, SET IN TYPE AND ASSEMBLED IN CANADA.
PRINTED IN ITALY / BOUND IN CANADA.